NAVIGATING THE SECRETS OF ALABAMA REAL ESTATE:
A Buyer's Guide in a Buyer Beware State

Mastering Home Purchases Amidst
Market Changes and New Regulations

Allison Click

DISCLAIMER

The information contained in this book, "Navigating The Secrets of Alabama Real Estate: A Buyer's Guide in a Buyer Beware State," is intended for educational and informational purposes only. It is designed to provide general guidance and to help buyers navigate the complexities of the real estate market in Alabama, particularly in light of the state's "buyer beware" laws and recent changes following the NAR settlement. However, it is not a substitute for professional advice.

PROFESSIONAL CONSULTATION

We strongly recommend that you consult with relevant professionals, including real estate agents, attorneys, home inspectors, and financial advisors, before making any real estate transactions. The advice and strategies outlined in this book are based on general real estate practices and may not be applicable to every individual situation.

ACCURACY OF INFORMATION

While every effort has been made to ensure the accuracy and completeness of the information presented, the author and publisher make no guarantees regarding the outcomes you may experience. Real estate laws and market conditions can change, and the information provided may become outdated or may not apply to specific circumstances.

NO LEGAL OR FINANCIAL LIABILITY

The author and publisher disclaim any liability for any direct, indirect, or consequential loss or damage incurred by any individual or entity relying on the information contained in this book. This includes, but is not limited to, errors or omissions, loss of data, loss of income, or any other losses resulting from the use or misuse of the information provided.

PERSONAL RESPONSIBILITY

Readers are encouraged to perform their own due diligence and to verify any information before making real estate decisions. This book should be used as a starting point for understanding the real estate market in Alabama and should not be relied upon as the sole source of information.

EXTERNAL LINKS AND REFERENCES

This book may contain references to third-party websites and resources. These links are provided for convenience and informational purposes only. The author and publisher do not endorse, guarantee, or assume responsibility for the accuracy or reliability of any information, products, or services offered by third-party websites.

By using this book, you acknowledge and agree to this disclaimer and assume full responsibility for your real estate decisions.

ABOUT THE AUTHOR

Allison Click is a seasoned real estate professional with years of experience in the Alabama real estate market. While this book draws on extensive industry knowledge and practical insights, it is intended as a guide to assist and inform buyers rather than replace professional advice.

TABLE OF CONTENTS

Section Name	Page
Foreward by Joe Stumpf	4
Introduction	7
What You'll Gain from this Book	8
Chapter Outline	10
Chapter 1: Introduction to Buyer Beware	13
Chapter 2: Understanding the Home Inspection	17
Chapter 3: Room-By-Room Guide for Buyers	24
Chapter 4: Major Systems and Structures	32
Chapter 5: Navigating the Real Estate Market	41
Chapter 6: Legal and Financial Preparedness	46
Conclusion: Why Choose Allison Click	51

FOREWARD

It is with great pleasure that I introduce this remarkable book, "Navigating The Secrets of Alabama Real Estate: A Buyer's Guide in a Buyer Beware State," authored by Allison Click. I have had the privilege of being Allison's business coach and witnessing her evolution into an extraordinary real estate professional. Over the past 15 years, Allison has been an invaluable member of our community, contributing, guiding, and leading with unwavering enthusiasm and dedication.

Allison's journey in the real estate world is nothing short of inspiring. Her deep commitment to helping others navigate the complexities of the Alabama real estate market is evident on every page of this book. She has crafted a comprehensive guide that empowers buyers with the knowledge and tools needed to make informed decisions in a state known for its "buyer beware" laws. This book is not just a compilation of information; it is a testament to Allison's character, her passion for real estate, and her unwavering desire to protect and educate her clients.

In the first chapter, you will delve into the concept of "buyer beware" and its critical importance in the Alabama real estate market. Allison meticulously explains the recent changes brought about by the NAR settlement and the implications for buyers. She emphasizes the invaluable role of a buyer's agent in safeguarding your interests, sharing compelling case studies that highlight the stark differences between informed and uninformed buyers.

The second chapter takes you through the essentials of home inspections, a crucial step in the home-buying process. Allison's insights into the key areas of inspection, from structural integrity to environmental hazards, are both practical and enlightening.

She underscores the importance of hiring certified inspectors and interpreting their reports accurately to make sound decisions.

In the third chapter, Allison provides a room-by-room guide for buyers, offering detailed advice on what to look for and how to prioritize improvements. Her recommendations, ranging from modernizing kitchens to enhancing outdoor spaces, reflect her keen understanding of what adds value to a home.

The fourth chapter focuses on major systems and structures, guiding you through the inspection and maintenance of crucial components such as the roof, foundation, and HVAC system. Allison's expertise shines as she explains how to identify potential issues and maintain these systems effectively to ensure the longevity and safety of your investment.

Navigating the real estate market is the theme of the fifth chapter, where Allison offers invaluable tips on understanding market conditions, making strategic decisions, and timing your transactions. Her insights into buyer's and seller's markets, local market trends, and working with real estate agents provide a solid foundation for making informed choices.

In the sixth chapter, Allison delves into the legal and financial aspects of real estate transactions. She outlines essential steps, from securing mortgage pre-approval to understanding purchase agreements and closing processes. Her guidance on budgeting for upfront and ongoing costs, as well as working with professionals, ensures you are fully prepared to handle the complexities of buying or selling a home.

Allison Click's dedication to her clients and her passion for real estate are the driving forces behind this book. Her expertise, combined with her genuine care for those she serves, makes her a trusted guide in the Alabama real estate market. This book is a reflection of who Allison is—a protector, a leader, and an enthusiastic advocate for her clients.

As you embark on your journey through "Navigating The Secrets of Alabama Real Estate: A Buyer's Guide in a Buyer Beware State," you will find yourself equipped with the knowledge and confidence to make sound decisions. Allison's wisdom and experience will be your companion, guiding you every step of the way.

Joe Stumpf
Business Coach By Referral Only

INTRODUCTION

Are you considering buying a home in Alabama? Before you sign anything, there's one critical resource you can't afford to miss: "Navigating The Secrets of Alabama Real Estate: A Buyer's Guide in a Buyer Beware State."

This indispensable guide is your key to making informed, confident decisions in one of the most complex real estate markets in the country. Here's why you need to read this book before making any commitments – and the costly mistakes you could avoid by doing so.

The Hidden Pitfalls of Alabama's Buyer Beware Market

Alabama operates under a "buyer beware" law, which means the responsibility to uncover property defects falls squarely on the buyer. Sellers are not legally obligated to disclose all known issues, leaving you vulnerable to hidden problems that could cost you thousands of dollars down the line. Imagine discovering structural issues, mold infestations, or faulty wiring only after you've moved in – problems that could have been avoided with the right knowledge and preparation.

The Impact of the NAR Settlement

The recent National Association of Realtors (NAR) settlement has shifted the financial landscape for buyers. You may now be responsible for your buyer's agent commission, adding an unexpected burden to your budget. Understanding these changes and how to navigate them is crucial. Our guide breaks down the implications of this settlement, helping you prepare financially and avoid unpleasant surprises.

WHAT YOU'LL GAIN FROM THIS BOOK

1. Comprehensive Understanding:
- Learn the intricacies of Alabama's buyer beware laws and how to protect yourself.
- Understand the new financial responsibilities brought by the NAR settlement.

2. Expert Strategies:
- Detailed room-by-room inspection checklists to ensure no detail is overlooked.
- Tips for negotiating with sellers to get the best possible deal.

3. Financial Preparedness:
- Budgeting tips to accommodate new commission structures and other costs.
- Insight into various financing options to make informed decisions.

4. Legal Safeguards:
- Essential information on the legal documents and procedures involved in buying a home.
- Guidance on hiring and working with real estate professionals to ensure you're protected.

THE COST OF IGNORANCE

Failing to educate yourself about Alabama's unique real estate challenges can lead to disastrous outcomes. Without this guide, you risk:

- **Financial Losses:** Unanticipated repair costs for issues like foundation cracks, roof leaks, or outdated electrical systems could drain your savings.

- **Legal Troubles:** Without understanding the necessary legal precautions, you might face legal disputes over undisclosed property issues.

- **Missed Opportunities:** Inability to navigate the new commission landscape could limit your purchasing power or cause you to miss out on your dream home.

WHY THIS BOOK IS ESSENTIAL

Real-Life Scenarios
The book includes real-life case studies illustrating the successes and failures of past buyers. Learn from their experiences to avoid making the same mistakes.

Professional Guidance
Written with input from leading real estate experts, including top agent Allison Click, this guide offers professional insights you won't find anywhere else.

Actionable Advice
Step-by-step strategies to guide you through every stage of the buying process, from initial search to closing the deal.

DON'T TAKE THE RISK – EQUIP YOURSELF WITH KNOWLEDGE

Before you make one of the biggest financial decisions of your life, ensure you're fully prepared. "Navigating The Secrets of Alabama Real Estate: A Buyer's Guide in a Buyer Beware State" is your essential companion in this journey. Empower yourself with the knowledge and strategies to make smart, confident decisions. Don't let ignorance cost you – invest in this guide today and navigate Alabama's real estate market with confidence and peace of mind.

CHAPTER 1: INTRODUCTION TO BUYER BEWARE

- Overview of Buyer Beware Concept: Importance in the current real estate market.

- Impact of the NAR Settlement: Explanation of changes and how they affect buyers.

- Importance of a Buyer's Agent: Role of buyer's agents in protecting buyers' interests.

- Case Studies: Two contrasting stories – one buyer with an agent, one without.

CHAPTER 2: UNDERSTANDING THE HOME INSPECTION

- Home Inspection Basics: What it is and why it's crucial.

- Key Areas of Inspection: Structural integrity, mold, termites, lead-based paint, radon.

- Common Oversights: Real-life examples of missed issues.

- Value of Professional Help: Importance of hiring certified inspectors.

CHAPTER 3: ROOM-BY-ROOM GUIDE FOR BUYERS

- Bedrooms: Popcorn ceilings, flooring, blinds, and more.

- Do's and Don'ts: Investments that pay off versus those that don't.

- Bathrooms: Mirrors, toilets, cabinets, and more.

- Renovation Tips: Enhancing value without over investing.

- Living/Family Rooms: Fireplaces, lighting, flooring.

- Modernization Tips: Simple updates for big impacts.

- Kitchens: Cabinets, hardware, appliances.

- Upgrade Strategies: Balancing personal enjoyment with future resale.

CHAPTER 4: EXTERIOR CONSIDERATIONS

- Landscaping: Mulch, plants, and curb appeal.

- Fencing: Privacy fences and their true value.

- Patios and Decks: Maintenance and upgrades.

- Cost-Effective Improvements: Pressure washing, staining, minor repairs.

CHAPTER 5: MAJOR SYSTEMS AND STRUCTURES

- Windows and Doors: Energy efficiency and aesthetics.

- HVAC Systems: Importance of modern systems and maintenance.

- Roofs and Foundations: Critical areas often overlooked.

- Long-Term Investments: Why some upgrades should be done early.

CHAPTER 6: NAVIGATING THE REAL ESTATE MARKET

- Buyer Beware States: What it means for buyers.

- Negotiation Strategies: Working with sellers and agents.

- Legal and Financial Preparedness: Ensuring all bases are covered.

- Final Walkthroughs and Closing: Last-minute checks and securing your investment.

CONCLUSION: EMPOWERED BUYING

- Recap of Key Points: Emphasizing the importance of awareness and professional guidance.

- Encouraging Proactive Decisions: Taking control of your home buying journey.

- Resources and Contacts: Additional reading, trusted inspectors, and agents.

CHAPTER 1:
Introduction to Buyer Beware

In the evolving landscape of real estate, the phrase "buyer beware" has never been more pertinent. This book aims to equip you with the knowledge and tools to navigate the complexities of home buying, ensuring that you make informed decisions and avoid common pitfalls. The recent National Association of Realtors (NAR) settlement has brought significant changes, particularly regarding how buyer's agents are compensated. Understanding these changes is crucial for anyone entering the real estate market today.

The Impact of the NAR Settlement

The NAR settlement has reshaped the way commissions are handled in real estate transactions. Traditionally, the seller paid the commission for both their agent and the buyer's agent. This arrangement is no longer a given, and buyers now need to be prepared to pay their agent's commission. This shift places a new financial burden on buyers, many of whom might be tempted to forego hiring an agent altogether. However, navigating the real estate market without professional guidance can be risky.

The settlement's intention is to foster transparency and fairness, but it also means that buyers must be more financially prepared and astute. The days of relying on the seller to cover these costs are waning, necessitating a shift in how buyers approach their home purchase budgets. It's imperative to recognize that while you might save on commission fees by not using an agent, the potential costs of making uninformed decisions can far outweigh these savings.

The Role of a Buyer's Agent

A buyer's agent plays a critical role in safeguarding your interests. They are your advocate, negotiator, and advisor, guiding you through every step of the buying process. From identifying potential issues in a property to negotiating the best price, their expertise can save you from costly mistakes.

One of the most significant advantages of having a buyer's agent is their access to market data and property histories. They can provide insights that are not readily available to the general public, helping you make informed decisions. Moreover, their experience in handling contracts and understanding legal obligations ensures that you are fully protected throughout the transaction.

CASE STUDY 1: The Informed Buyer

Consider the story of Sarah, a first-time homebuyer. Sarah understood the importance of having a buyer's agent and enlisted the help of a seasoned professional. Her agent recommended a thorough home inspection, which revealed significant mold issues in the crawl space—an issue that Sarah would not have identified on her own. The agent negotiated with the seller to cover the cost of remediation, saving Sarah thousands of dollars and ensuring her new home was safe.

CASE STUDY 2: The Uninformed Buyer

Contrast this with the experience of John, who decided to forgo hiring an agent to save on commission fees. John found a property he liked and, without a professional's guidance, did not conduct a home inspection. After moving in, he discovered severe structural issues and mold in the basement. The cost of repairs was substantial, and because he had not documented these issues before closing, he had no recourse against the seller. John's attempt to save a few thousand dollars ended up costing him much more in the long run.

Understanding the Home Inspection

A comprehensive home inspection is one of the most critical steps in the home buying process. It's an opportunity to uncover hidden problems that could affect the safety, livability, and value of the property. A qualified inspector will examine everything from the foundation to the roof, including plumbing, electrical systems, and potential environmental hazards like mold or radon.

In Alabama, a buyer beware state, the onus is on the buyer to identify and address any issues with the property before closing. This makes the home inspection even more crucial. A buyer's agent will recommend reputable inspectors and ensure that all potential problems are thoroughly investigated. They will also help you interpret the inspection report and negotiate with the seller to address any significant issues.

The Importance of Disclosure

While sellers are required to disclose known defects in many states, this is not always the case in buyer beware states like Alabama. Even in states with disclosure requirements, there are often gray areas, and some sellers may not fully disclose all issues. This is where a buyer's agent can provide invaluable assistance, asking the right questions and ensuring that you are aware of all potential concerns.

Making Informed Decisions

The goal of this book is to empower you to make informed decisions throughout the home buying process. By understanding the potential pitfalls and knowing what to look for, you can avoid costly mistakes and ensure that your investment is sound. Whether it's understanding the implications of the NAR settlement, recognizing the value of a thorough home inspection, or appreciating the role of a buyer's agent, knowledge is your best defense in the real estate market.

In the chapters that follow, we will delve deeper into each aspect of the home buying process, providing you with detailed, practical advice. From room-by-room guides to understanding major systems and structures, this book will be your comprehensive resource for making smart, informed decisions. Remember, while the changes in the real estate landscape might seem daunting, with the right knowledge and guidance, you can navigate this market successfully. Welcome to the world of informed buying—welcome to Buyer Beware.

CHAPTER 2:
Understanding the Home Inspection

A home inspection is a crucial part of the home buying process, offering you a detailed understanding of the property you intend to purchase. It can reveal hidden problems that might not be immediately obvious, ensuring that you make an informed decision. This chapter will guide you through the importance of home inspections, what to expect during the process, and how to effectively use the inspection report to your advantage.

THE PURPOSE OF A HOME INSPECTION

The primary purpose of a home inspection is to identify any existing or potential issues with the property. A thorough inspection provides a detailed analysis of the home's condition, including its structure, systems, and components. This helps you avoid costly surprises after the purchase and gives you leverage in negotiating repairs or price reductions with the seller.

An inspection typically covers the following areas:

- **Structural Components:** Foundations, beams, and columns.
- **Roofing:** Condition of shingles, gutters, and any signs of leaks.
- **Electrical Systems:** Wiring, outlets, and service panels.
- **Plumbing:** Pipes, fixtures, and water heaters.
- **HVAC Systems:** Heating, ventilation, and air conditioning.
- **Interior and Exterior:** Walls, ceilings, windows, doors, and overall safety concerns.
- **Insulation and Ventilation:** Ensuring energy efficiency and proper air flow.

- **Major Appliances:** Functionality and safety of kitchen and laundry appliances.
- **Environmental Hazards:** Checking for mold, radon, and other potential health risks.

SELECTING A QUALIFIED INSPECTOR

Choosing a qualified and experienced home inspector is critical. Your real estate agent can recommend reputable inspectors, but you should also do your own research. Look for inspectors who are certified by professional organizations such as the American Society of Home Inspectors (ASHI) or the International Association of Certified Home Inspectors (InterNACHI). Certification ensures that the inspector adheres to high standards of practice and ethics.

When interviewing potential inspectors, consider the following:

- **Experience:** How long have they been in business and how many inspections have they completed?
- **Credentials:** Are they certified and licensed, if required by your state?
- **References:** Can they provide testimonials or references from past clients?
- **Sample Reports:** Review a sample inspection report to ensure it is thorough and easy to understand.
- **Insurance:** Do they carry professional liability insurance, also known as Errors and Omissions (E&O) insurance?

Preparing for the Inspection

Once you've selected an inspector, schedule the inspection as soon as possible after your offer is accepted. Ideally, you should be present during the inspection to ask questions and gain firsthand understanding of any issues. This also allows the inspector to explain the severity and implications of any findings in real time.

Before the inspection, prepare a checklist of any specific concerns or areas you want the inspector to focus on. Provide the inspector with access to all areas of the home, including the attic, basement, and crawl spaces. Ensure that utilities are turned on so the inspector can test the electrical system, plumbing, and appliances.

THE INSPECTION PROCESS

A typical home inspection takes two to four hours, depending on the size and condition of the property. The inspector will methodically examine each aspect of the home, taking notes and photographs to document their findings. Here's a breakdown of what to expect during the inspection:

1. Exterior Inspection

The inspector will start by examining the exterior of the home, including the foundation, siding, windows, and doors. They will look for signs of damage, wear, and potential water intrusion.

2. Roof Inspection

Next, the inspector will assess the condition of the roof, including shingles, flashing, and gutters. They will check for any signs of leaks or damage.

3. Interior Inspection

Moving inside, the inspector will examine the walls, ceilings, floors, and stairs. They will look for cracks, stains, or other signs of structural issues or water damage.

4. Electrical Systems

The inspector will test outlets, switches, and the main service panel. They will check for proper grounding, overloaded circuits, and any outdated or hazardous wiring.

5. Plumbing
The inspector will check the water pressure, look for leaks, and assess the condition of pipes and fixtures. They will also inspect the water heater for age and functionality.

6. HVAC Systems
The heating and cooling systems will be tested to ensure they are working properly. The inspector will also check for adequate insulation and ventilation.

7. Attic and Basement
These areas are crucial for identifying potential structural issues, moisture problems, and proper insulation.

8. Environmental Hazards
If applicable, the inspector will test for mold, radon, asbestos, and other environmental hazards that could affect your health.

UNDERSTANDING THE INSPECTION REPORT

After the inspection, the inspector will provide a detailed report outlining their findings. This report typically includes:

- **Summary of Major Issues:** A list of the most critical problems that need immediate attention.

- **Detailed Descriptions:** In-depth explanations of each issue, including photographs and recommendations for repairs.

- **Maintenance Tips:** Suggestions for routine maintenance to keep the home in good condition.

- **Safety Concerns:** Identification of any potential safety hazards.

USING THE INSPECTION REPORT

The inspection report is a powerful tool for negotiating with the seller. If the inspection reveals significant issues, you have several options:

- **Request Repairs:** Ask the seller to make the necessary repairs before closing.

- **Seek a Price Reduction:** Negotiate a lower purchase price to cover the cost of repairs.

- **Request a Credit:** Ask for a credit at closing to cover future repair costs.

- **Walk Away:** If the issues are too severe, you may choose to back out of the deal, provided your contract includes an inspection contingency.

It's important to prioritize the findings in the report. Focus on major issues that affect the safety, structural integrity, and habitability of the home. Minor cosmetic issues or routine maintenance items should not be deal-breakers.

THE ROLE OF YOUR BUYER'S AGENT

Your buyer's agent is an invaluable resource during this process. They can help you understand the inspection report, prioritize repairs, and negotiate with the seller. Their experience and knowledge can prevent you from making costly mistakes and ensure that you get the best possible deal.

For example, your agent can guide you in selecting reputable contractors to provide estimates for repairs. They can also help you determine which repairs are essential and which ones can be addressed later. This strategic approach ensures that you are not overwhelmed by the inspection report and can make informed decisions about your purchase.

COMMON ISSUES FOUND DURING INSPECTIONS

Home inspections often uncover a variety of issues, some more common than others. Here are a few typical problems inspectors encounter:

- **Roofing Problems**
  Leaks, missing shingles, and damaged flashing are common issues that can lead to significant water damage if not addressed.

- **Electrical Issues**
  Outdated wiring, overloaded circuits, and lack of proper grounding are frequent findings that pose fire hazards.

- **Plumbing Leaks**
  Leaking pipes, fixtures, and water heaters can cause water damage and mold growth.

- **Foundation Cracks**
  Minor cracks are normal, but significant foundation issues can affect the structural integrity of the home.

- **HVAC System Failures**
  Inefficient or malfunctioning heating and cooling systems can lead to high energy bills and discomfort.

- **Mold and Mildew**
  High moisture levels in basements and crawl spaces often lead to mold growth, which can be a health hazard.

THE POWER OF KNOWLEDGE

A home inspection is an investment in your future. It provides peace of mind, ensures that you are aware of any potential problems, and gives you the information you need to make an informed decision. By understanding the inspection process and effectively utilizing the inspection report, you can navigate the home buying process with confidence.

In the next chapter, we will delve into a room-by-room guide, offering practical advice on what to look for and how to prioritize improvements. Remember, knowledge is your best defense in the real estate market. Stay informed, stay vigilant, and always be prepared to make the best decisions for your future home.

CHAPTER 3:
Room-by-Room Guide for Buyers

When buying a home, it's essential to scrutinize every room to ensure you're making a sound investment. Each room in a house serves a unique purpose and comes with its own set of potential issues and improvements. This chapter will provide a detailed room-by-room guide, highlighting what to look for during your inspection and offering advice on which improvements will yield the best returns.

BEDROOMS

Bedrooms are private sanctuaries, and their condition can significantly affect a home's appeal and value. Here are key aspects to consider:

- Popcorn Ceilings

Many older homes have popcorn ceilings, which can be unattractive and difficult to maintain. Removing popcorn ceilings and smoothing them out can modernize the space and increase the home's appeal. Although this process can be messy and time-consuming, it's often worth the investment, as smooth ceilings are more desirable.

- Flooring

Inspect the condition of the bedroom floors. Hardwood floors are highly sought after for their durability and aesthetic appeal. If the home has carpet, consider its age and condition. Replacing old, stained carpet with new carpet or upgrading to hardwood or laminate flooring can significantly boost the room's appeal.

- **Window Treatments**
  Quality window treatments can enhance a bedroom's look and functionality. Blinds or shutters provide privacy and light control, while curtains can add a touch of style. Opt for neutral colors that will appeal to a wide range of buyers.

- **Closet Space**
  Adequate closet space is a major selling point. Check the closets for functionality and size. Simple upgrades like installing organizers or additional shelving can make a big difference.

- **Lighting**
  Proper lighting is crucial. Ensure there are sufficient light fixtures and that they are up-to-date. Adding a ceiling fan with a light or modern light fixtures can improve the room's ambiance and functionality.

BATHROOMS

Bathrooms are critical in determining a home's value and desirability. Buyers pay close attention to the condition and style of bathrooms, so here's what to focus on:

- **Fixtures and Fittings**
  Modern fixtures can make a significant difference. Replacing old faucets, showerheads, and towel racks with contemporary designs can update the space at a relatively low cost.

- **Vanity and Storage**
  A new vanity with ample storage can improve both functionality and appearance. Opt for styles that provide plenty of counter space and storage without overwhelming the room.

- **Tiles and Grout**
Check for cracked or missing tiles and dirty or moldy grout. Replacing damaged tiles and cleaning or regrouting can freshen up the bathroom. Consider modern, neutral-colored tiles for a timeless look.

- **Mirrors and Lighting**
A large, framed mirror can enhance the sense of space. Ensure the bathroom has adequate lighting, particularly around the vanity area. LED lighting is a popular choice for its brightness and energy efficiency.

- **Toilets**
A modern, water-efficient toilet can be a worthwhile upgrade. It not only improves the bathroom's look but also saves water, which is appealing to eco-conscious buyers.

- **Bathtub and Shower**
Inspect the condition of the bathtub and shower. Any signs of mold or mildew should be addressed immediately. Consider reglazing an old bathtub or installing a new showerhead to update the space.

LIVING AND FAMILY ROOMS

These communal spaces are where families gather and entertain, making them a focal point in home buying decisions. Here's how to ensure they stand out:

- **Fireplace**
If the home has a fireplace, ensure it's in good working order and clean. Consider upgrading from a wood-burning to a gas fireplace for ease of use and efficiency.

- **Flooring**
  Hardwood floors are highly desirable in living spaces. If the room has carpet, consider its condition and whether replacing it with hardwood or laminate flooring would be beneficial.

- **Lighting**
  Good lighting is essential. Ensure the room has both natural light and adequate artificial lighting. Recessed lighting or a stylish ceiling fixture can enhance the space.

- **Walls and Paint**
  Neutral, fresh paint can make the room feel updated and welcoming. Avoid bold colors that may not appeal to all buyers.

- **Built-Ins and Storage**
  Built-in shelving or storage units can add both functionality and charm. Ensure these are in good condition and consider adding them if space allows.

KITCHENS

The kitchen is often considered the heart of the home and can be a major selling point. Here's how to ensure it impresses:

- **Cabinets**
  Inspect the condition of the cabinets. Painting or refacing old cabinets can be a cost-effective way to update the kitchen. Ensure the hardware is modern and consistent throughout.

- **Countertops**
  Countertops should be durable and attractive. Consider replacing laminate countertops with granite or quartz for a high-end look.

- **Appliances**
Modern, energy-efficient appliances are a major plus. Ensure all appliances are in good working order and match in style and color.

- **Backsplash**
A stylish backsplash can add character to the kitchen. Choose neutral or classic designs that will appeal to a broad audience.

- **Flooring**
Durable flooring, such as tile or hardwood, is preferred in kitchens. Ensure the flooring is in good condition and consider replacing outdated or worn materials.

- **Lighting**
Good lighting is essential for cooking and entertaining. Ensure there is adequate task lighting under cabinets and ambient lighting from ceiling fixtures.

DINING AREAS

Dining areas, whether formal dining rooms or casual breakfast nooks, should be inviting spaces. Here's how to enhance these areas:

- **Lighting**
A statement chandelier or pendant lights can add elegance and focus to the dining area. Ensure the lighting is appropriate for the size of the table and the room.

- **Wall Treatments**
Consider wainscoting or a fresh coat of paint to define the space. Neutral colors are best, but an accent wall can add interest without overwhelming the space.

- **Flooring**
  Durable, easy-to-clean flooring is important in dining areas. Hardwood or tile floors are preferable to carpet.

- **Space and Flow**
  Ensure the dining area feels spacious and easy to navigate. Avoid overcrowding with furniture, and ensure there's enough room for comfortable seating.

HOME OFFICES

With more people working from home, a functional home office can be a strong selling point. Here's how to make it stand out:

- **Desk and Storage**
  Ensure there's a suitable space for a desk and storage. Built-in shelving or cabinets can add value and functionality.

- **Lighting**
  Adequate lighting is crucial for a home office. Ensure there's plenty of natural light, as well as task lighting for work.

- **Soundproofing**
  Consider adding soundproofing elements, such as heavy curtains or area rugs, to create a quiet workspace.

- **Connectivity**
  Ensure the room has ample outlets and good internet connectivity. These are essential for a functional home office.

OUTDOOR AREAS

Outdoor living spaces can significantly enhance a home's appeal. Here's what to focus on:

- **Landscaping**
Well-maintained landscaping adds to the curb appeal. Consider fresh mulch, trimmed hedges, and colorful plants. Avoid overly complex landscaping that requires extensive maintenance.

- **Decks and Patios**
Inspect the condition of decks and patios. Ensure there are no rotten boards or loose railings. A fresh coat of stain or paint can rejuvenate the space.

- **Lighting**
Outdoor lighting enhances safety and ambiance. Consider installing pathway lights, deck lights, or string lights for a welcoming outdoor space.

- **Privacy Fences**
While a privacy fence might not always yield a high return, it can be important for buyers with pets or children. Ensure any existing fences are in good condition.

BASEMENTS AND ATTICS

These areas often house important systems and can be used for additional living space or storage. Here's what to inspect:

- **Moisture and Mold**
Check for any signs of moisture or mold. Addressing these issues promptly can prevent larger problems down the line.

- **Insulation**
Proper insulation is crucial for energy efficiency. Ensure the attic is well-insulated, and consider adding insulation if needed.

- **Structural Issues**
  Look for any cracks or signs of structural damage. These should be addressed immediately, as they can affect the integrity of the home.

- **Storage Solutions**
  Adding shelving or storage units can make these spaces more functional and appealing.

MAXIMIZING YOUR INVESTMENT

By carefully inspecting and updating each room in a home, you can significantly enhance its appeal and value. Focus on improvements that offer the best return on investment and address any major issues before they become costly problems. This room-by-room guide provides a comprehensive approach to ensuring your home is both beautiful and functional, making it a wise investment for the future.

In the next chapter, we will explore major systems and structures in more detail, providing further guidance on what to look for and how to maintain them. Remember, a well-maintained home not only provides a comfortable living environment but also protects your investment for years to come.

CHAPTER 4:
Major Systems and Structures

Understanding and maintaining the major systems and structures of a home is crucial for ensuring its longevity, safety, and value. These components are often the most expensive to repair or replace, so it's essential to inspect them thoroughly before purchasing a home. This chapter will guide you through the key systems and structures to focus on, what to look for during inspections, and how to maintain them effectively.

ROOF

The roof is one of the most critical components of a home. It protects the structure from weather elements and helps maintain the integrity of the building. Here's what to consider:

Inspection Tips:

- **Age and Material**
  Determine the age of the roof and the type of materials used. Asphalt shingles typically last 20-30 years, while metal roofs can last 40-70 years.

- **Signs of Damage**
  Look for missing, curling, or damaged shingles. Check for granule loss, which can indicate the roof is nearing the end of its life.

- **Leaks and Water Damage**
  Inspect the attic and ceilings for signs of water intrusion, such as stains or mold. Ensure gutters and downspouts are directing water away from the foundation.

Maintenance:

- Regular Inspections
Have a professional inspect the roof annually and after major storms.

- Cleaning
Keep gutters and downspouts clear of debris to prevent water backup and damage.

- Repairs
Address minor issues promptly to prevent them from becoming major problems.

FOUNDATION

The foundation supports the entire structure of the home, making it essential to its stability. Foundation issues can lead to significant structural problems if not addressed.

Inspection Tips:

- Cracks and Settling
Check for cracks in the foundation, walls, and floors. Minor hairline cracks are often normal, but larger cracks can indicate settling or structural issues.

- Water Damage
Look for signs of water damage, such as efflorescence (white mineral deposits) or dampness in the basement or crawl space.

- Doors and Windows
Ensure doors and windows open and close properly, as misalignment can indicate foundation movement.

Maintenance:

- **Proper Drainage**
Ensure the ground around the foundation slopes away from the home to prevent water accumulation.

- **Seal Cracks**
Seal minor cracks with appropriate materials to prevent water intrusion and further damage.

- **Professional Inspection**
Have a structural engineer inspect significant cracks or signs of settling to determine the necessary repairs.

ELECTRICAL SYSTEM

A home's electrical system is vital for safety and functionality. Faulty wiring can pose fire hazards, so it's essential to ensure the system is up to code and in good working order.

Inspection Tips:

- **Wiring and Panels**
Check for outdated wiring, such as knob-and-tube or aluminum wiring, which may need updating. Ensure the electrical panel is sufficient for the home's needs and free of rust or corrosion.

- **Outlets and Switches**
Test outlets and switches for proper functionality. Ensure there are enough outlets to meet modern electrical demands.

- **Ground Fault Circuit Interrupters (GFCIs)**
Verify that GFCIs are installed in areas with water exposure, such as kitchens, bathrooms, and outdoor outlets.

Maintenance:

- **Regular Inspections**
  Have a licensed electrician inspect the system periodically, especially in older homes.

- **Upgrade as Needed**
  Upgrade wiring, panels, and outlets to meet current safety standards and electrical demands.

- **Safe Practices**
  Avoid overloading circuits and use surge protectors to safeguard electronics.

PLUMBING SYSTEM

The plumbing system is essential for providing clean water and removing wastewater. Issues such as leaks or clogs can cause significant damage and health hazards.

Inspection Tips:

- **Pipes and Fittings**
  Check for leaks, corrosion, or outdated materials like lead or galvanized pipes, which may need replacement.

- **Water Heater**
  Inspect the age and condition of the water heater. Most water heaters last 10-15 years.

- **Fixtures and Drains**
  Test faucets, showers, and toilets for proper function. Ensure drains are clear and free of slow drainage or backups.

Maintenance:

- **Regular Inspections**
  Inspect the plumbing system annually for leaks, corrosion, and proper function.

- **Water Heater Maintenance**
  Flush the water heater annually to remove sediment buildup and extend its lifespan.

- **Preventative Measures**
  Insulate pipes in unheated areas to prevent freezing and bursting in cold weather.

HEATING, VENTILATION, AND AIR CONDITIONING (HVAC) SYSTEM

The HVAC system is critical for maintaining a comfortable and healthy indoor environment. Efficient heating and cooling can valso save on energy costs.

Inspection Tips:

- **Age and Efficiency**
  Determine the age and efficiency of the HVAC units. Systems older than 15-20 years may need replacement.

- **Airflow and Ductwork**
  Check for proper airflow and inspect ductwork for leaks, damage, or poor insulation.

- **Thermostat**
  Ensure the thermostat functions correctly and consider upgrading to a programmable or smart thermostat for better energy management.

Maintenance:

- **Regular Servicing**
  Have the HVAC system serviced by a professional twice a year—before the heating and cooling seasons.

- **Filter Replacement**
  Replace air filters every 1-3 months to maintain air quality and system efficiency.

- **Duct Cleaning**
  Clean ducts every few years to remove dust and allergens and ensure efficient airflow.

WINDOWS AND DOORS

Windows and doors are crucial for energy efficiency, security, and curb appeal. Proper maintenance can enhance their lifespan and performance.

Inspection Tips:

- **Condition and Fit**
  Check for drafts, broken seals, or gaps around windows and doors. Ensure they open and close smoothly.

- **Glass and Frames**
  Inspect for cracked or broken glass and damaged frames. Double-paned windows should be free of condensation between panes.

- **Locks and Hardware**
  Test locks and hardware for security and proper function.

Maintenance:

- Sealing and Caulking
Re-seal and caulk around windows and doors to prevent drafts and water intrusion.

- Cleaning
Clean windows and frames regularly to maintain appearance and function.

- Repair and Replace
Address minor repairs promptly and replace outdated or damaged windows and doors to improve energy efficiency and security.

INSULATION AND VENTILATION

Proper insulation and ventilation are key to maintaining a comfortable, energy-efficient home. They help regulate temperature, reduce energy costs, and prevent moisture problems.

Inspection Tips:

- Insulation Levels
Check the attic, walls, and floors for adequate insulation. Look for gaps, settling, or damage.

- Ventilation
Ensure proper ventilation in attics, crawl spaces, and bathrooms to prevent moisture buildup and mold growth.

- Air Sealing
Inspect for air leaks around windows, doors, and other openings.

Maintenance:

- **Upgrade Insulation**
  Add insulation where needed to meet current energy standards. Focus on attics and crawl spaces for the best return on investment.

- **Ventilation Maintenance**
  Clean and maintain vents and exhaust fans to ensure proper airflow.

- **Air Sealing**
  Seal gaps and cracks to improve energy efficiency and indoor comfort.

WATER MANAGEMENT SYSTEMS

Effective water management is crucial for preventing damage and maintaining the structural integrity of a home. This includes gutters, downspouts, and drainage systems.

Inspection Tips:

- **Gutters and Downspouts**
  Check for clogs, leaks, and proper attachment. Ensure downspouts direct water away from the foundation.

- **Drainage**
  Inspect the property for proper grading and drainage. Look for areas where water pools or flows toward the house.

- **Basement and Crawl Space**
  Check for signs of moisture or water intrusion, such | as dampness, mold, or musty odors.

Maintenance:

- **Regular Cleaning**
Clean gutters and downspouts at least twice a year to prevent clogs and water damage.

- **Repair and Replace**
Repair any damaged gutters or downspouts promptly. Consider installing gutter guards to reduce maintenance.

- **Improve Drainage**
Ensure proper grading around the foundation and install drainage solutions, such as French drains or sump pumps, if necessary.

The Foundation of a Sound Investment

Maintaining the major systems and structures of a home is essential for ensuring its safety, comfort, and value. By thoroughly inspecting these components before purchase and committing to regular maintenance, you can prevent costly repairs and extend the lifespan of your home.

In the next chapter, we will explore the importance of understanding the local real estate market and how to make informed decisions based on market trends and conditions. Remember, a well-maintained home is not only a more enjoyable place to live but also a more valuable investment. Stay proactive, stay informed, and your home will continue to serve you well for years to come.

CHAPTER 5:
Navigating the Real Estate Market

Understanding the local real estate market is crucial for making informed decisions when buying or selling a home. Market conditions can significantly impact property values, negotiation power, and the overall buying or selling experience. This chapter will provide insights into navigating the real estate market, understanding market trends, and making strategic decisions based on current conditions.

Understanding Market Conditions

Real estate markets are influenced by various factors, including economic conditions, interest rates, and local supply and demand. Being aware of these factors can help you make better decisions.

BUYER'S MARKET VS. SELLER'S MARKET:

- **Buyer's Market**
  In a buyer's market, there are more homes for sale than there are buyers. This excess supply gives buyers the upper hand, as sellers may be more willing to negotiate on price and terms. Indicators of a buyer's market include longer days on the market, price reductions, and an increase in available listings.

- **Seller's Market**
  Conversely, in a seller's market, there are more buyers than available homes. This high demand often leads to competitive bidding, higher prices, and quicker sales. Indicators of a seller's market include short days on the market, multiple offers, and rising home prices.

RESEARCHING LOCAL MARKET TRENDS

To make informed decisions, it's essential to research and understand local market trends. Here's how to gather and interpret market data:

- **Real Estate Listings**
Regularly review listings in your target area to get a sense of what's available and at what price. Pay attention to the listing history, such as price changes and time on the market.

- **Market Reports**
Many real estate websites and local agencies publish monthly or quarterly market reports. These reports provide valuable data on average sale prices, inventory levels, and market trends.

- **Comparable Sales**
Look at recently sold homes similar to the one you're interested in. This will give you a realistic idea of the current market value and help you set competitive offers or listing prices.

- **Economic Indicators**
Stay informed about broader economic conditions, such as interest rates, employment rates, and local economic developments. These factors can influence market trends and buyer behavior.

MAKING STRATEGIC DECISIONS

Whether you're buying or selling, making strategic decisions based on market conditions can enhance your success. Here are some tips for both buyers and sellers:

For Buyers:

- **Set a Budget**
  Determine your budget based on your financial situation and stick to it. Factor in potential market fluctuations and vinterest rate changes.

- **Be Prepared to Act Quickly**
  In a seller's market, desirable homes can sell quickly. Have your financing pre-approved and be ready to make a swift decision.

- **Negotiate Wisely**
  In a buyer's market, you have more room to negotiate. Don't be afraid to ask for repairs, concessions, or a lower price. In a seller's market, consider making a strong initial offer to stand out.

For Sellers:

- **Price Strategically**
  Setting the right price is crucial. Overpricing can lead to extended time on the market and eventual price reductions. Use comparable sales and market trends to set a competitive price.

- **Enhance Curb Appeal**
  First impressions matter. Invest in landscaping, paint, and minor repairs to make your home more appealing to potential buyers.

- **Stage Your Home**
  Staging can help buyers envision themselves in the space. Consider hiring a professional stager or follow DIY staging tips to highlight your home's best features.

WORKING WITH A REAL ESTATE AGENT

A knowledgeable real estate agent can be an invaluable asset in navigating the market. Here's how an agent can assist you:

- **Market Expertise**
Agents have access to comprehensive market data and can provide insights that are not readily available to the public. They can help you understand current trends, set realistic expectations, and make informed decisions.

- **Negotiation Skills**
Experienced agents are skilled negotiators. They can advocate on your behalf, whether you're buying or selling, to ensure you get the best possible deal.

- **Network and Resources**
Agents have a network of professionals, including lenders, inspectors, and contractors, which can streamline the buying or selling process.

- **Handling Paperwork**
Real estate transactions involve significant paperwork and legal considerations. An agent can manage these details, ensuring that all documents are correctly completed and submitted.

TIMING THE MARKET

While it can be challenging to predict market fluctuations, understanding seasonal trends can help you time your purchase or sale more effectively.

Spring and Summer: These seasons are typically the busiest for real estate, with more listings and higher buyer activity. Homes often sell faster and at higher prices during these months.

Fall and Winter: The market tends to slow down in the fall and winter, with fewer listings and buyers. However, this can be an opportunity for buyers to find deals, as sellers may be more motivated to sell before the year ends.

CONCLUSION: Making Informed Decisions

Navigating the real estate market requires knowledge, preparation, and strategic decision-making. By understanding market conditions, researching trends, and working with a skilled real estate agent, you can make informed decisions that align with your goals.

In the next chapter, we will explore the importance of legal and financial preparedness, ensuring you are fully equipped to handle the complexities of real estate transactions. Remember, staying informed and proactive will help you navigate the market with confidence and achieve the best possible outcomes.

CHAPTER 6:
Legal and Financial Preparedness

Entering the real estate market requires not only understanding the physical aspects of a property but also being prepared for the legal and financial complexities of buying or selling a home. This chapter will cover essential steps and considerations to ensure you are fully equipped to handle these aspects, minimizing risks and maximizing benefits.

LEGAL ASPECTS OF REAL ESTATE TRANSACTIONS

Real estate transactions involve numerous legal documents and procedures. Here's a breakdown of key legal elements you need to be aware of:

Purchase Agreement

- **Definition**
  A legally binding contract between the buyer and seller outlining the terms of the sale.

- **Key Components**
  Purchase price, closing date, contingencies (such as inspections or financing), and details about what is included in the sale.

- **Review**
  Have a real estate attorney review the agreement to ensure all terms are clear and in your best interest.

Title Search and Insurance

- **Title Search**
  Conducted to verify the seller's legal right to sell the property

and to check for any liens, encumbrances, or other issues that could affect ownership.

- **Title Insurance**
Protects against future claims or disputes over property ownership. It's a one-time fee that offers long-term protection.

Disclosure Requirements

- **Sellers' Obligations**
Sellers are typically required to disclose known issues with the property. This can include structural problems, environmental hazards, and other material defects.

- **Buyers' Rights**
As a buyer, ensure you receive and review all disclosures to understand any potential issues before completing the purchase.

Closing Process

- **Final Walkthrough**
Conduct a final inspection of the property to ensure it is vin the agreed-upon condition.

- **Closing Statement**
Review the closing statement (also known as the HUD-1 Settlement Statement) to understand all fees and charges associated with the transaction.

- **Signing Documents**
Sign all necessary documents, including the deed, loan documents, and any other paperwork required to finalize the sale.

FINANCIAL PREPAREDNESS

Being financially prepared is crucial for a smooth real estate transaction. Here are key financial considerations and steps:

Pre-Approval for Mortgage

- **Importance**

  Getting pre-approved for a mortgage shows sellers you are a serious buyer and gives you a clear understanding of your budget.

- **Process**

  Provide financial documents to your lender, such as income statements, tax returns, and credit reports, to get pre-approved.

Budgeting for Upfront Costs

- **Down Payment**

  Typically 3% to 20% of the purchase price, depending on the type of mortgage and lender requirements.

- **Closing Costs**

  Usually 2% to 5% of the loan amount, covering fees for appraisal, title insurance, attorney fees, and more.

- **Moving Expenses**

  Include costs for moving services, utilities setup, and any immediate repairs or upgrades needed in your new home.

Ongoing Homeownership Costs

- **Mortgage Payments**

  Principal, interest, property taxes, and homeowners insurance.

- **Maintenance and Repairs**

  Budget for regular maintenance and unexpected repairs.

- **Utilities and HOA Fees**
  Monthly costs for utilities and any homeowners association fees if applicable.

Financial Contingencies in the Purchase Agreement

- **Inspection Contingency**
  Allows you to back out of the deal if significant issues are found during the home inspection.

- **Appraisal Contingency**
  Ensures the property appraises for at least the purchase price.

- **Financing Contingency**
  Protects you if you are unable to secure financing.

WORKING WITH PROFESSIONALS

Having a team of professionals can make the legal and financial aspects of real estate transactions more manageable:

Real Estate Attorney

- **Role:** Provides legal advice, reviews contracts, and ensures all legal aspects of the transaction are handled properly.

- **When to Hire:** Consider hiring an attorney for complex transactions, such as those involving commercial properties or significant financial investment.

Mortgage Broker

- **Role:** Helps you find the best mortgage terms and rates by comparing offers from multiple lenders.

- **Benefits:** Can save you time and money by negotiating on your behalf and guiding you through the loan application process.

Home Inspector

- **Role:** Conducts a thorough inspection of the property to identify any potential issues.

- **Benefits:** Provides a detailed report that can be used to negotiate repairs or price reductions with the seller.

CONCLUSION: The Importance of Preparation

Legal and financial preparedness is essential for a successful real estate transaction. By understanding the key aspects of real estate law, budgeting appropriately, and working with knowledgeable professionals, you can navigate the complexities of buying or selling a home with confidence.

CONCLUSION:
WHY CHOOSE ALLISON CLICK

When it comes to real estate in Huntsville, Alabama, Allison Click stands out as a premier agent, offering unparalleled expertise and dedication. With years of experience and a deep understanding of the local market, Allison provides personalized and professional service to both buyers and sellers.

Expertise and Experience
Allison Click is affiliated with Leading Edge Real Estate Group, where she has established a reputation for excellence. Her comprehensive knowledge of the Huntsville market, combined with her commitment to staying current with real estate trends and technologies, ensures that her clients receive the best possible advice and support.

Personalized Service
Allison is known for her responsiveness and attention to detail. She takes the time to understand each client's unique needs and goals, tailoring her approach to ensure a smooth and successful transaction. Whether you're a first-time homebuyer or an experienced investor, Allison's personalized service will guide you every step of the way.

Proven Track Record
With numerous positive reviews and a track record of successful sales, Allison has proven her ability to deliver results. Her clients consistently praise her professionalism, market knowledge, and dedication to achieving their real estate objectives.

Comprehensive Support

Allison offers a full range of services, from market analysis and property searches to negotiation and closing support. She also provides valuable resources and recommendations for home inspections, financing, and legal assistance, ensuring that her clients have everything they need to make informed decisions.

For anyone looking to buy or sell a home in Huntsville, Alabama, Allison Click is the ideal choice. Her expertise, personalized service, and commitment to excellence make her a trusted partner in the real estate process. By choosing Allison, you can be confident that you are working with one of the best agents in the area, dedicated to helping you achieve your real estate goals.

Copyright © 2024 by Allison Click

All rights reserved.

No portion of this book may be reproduced in any form without written permission from the publisher or author, except as permitted by U.S. copyright law.

ISBN: 9798332869501

www.ingramcontent.com/pod-product-compliance
Lightning Source LLC
Chambersburg PA
CBHW072019230526
45479CB00008B/294